The Wet Life

Dr. Jasleen Kaur

Copyright © Dr. Jasleen Kaur 2024
All Rights Reserved.

ISBN
Paperback 979-8-89498-376-9
Hardcase 979-8-89498-856-6

This book has been published with all efforts taken to make the material error-free after the consent of the author. However, the author and the publisher do not assume and hereby disclaim any liability to any party for any loss, damage, or disruption caused by errors or omissions, whether such errors or omissions result from negligence, accident, or any other cause.

While every effort has been made to avoid any mistake or omission, this publication is being sold on the condition and understanding that neither the author nor the publishers or printers would be liable in any manner to any person by reason of any mistake or omission in this publication or for any action taken or omitted to be taken or advice rendered or accepted on the basis of this work. For any defect in printing or binding the publishers will be liable only to replace the defective copy by another copy of this work then available.

Dedicated to Perrito

(25th January 2009 – 18th May 2024),

my little angel who accompanied

me from my first year in

Vet school, right to my first year of MBA

and taught me so much of what I know

about paw-renthood.

Being veterinarians,
we're not supposed to be afraid of any
animals. And I'm afraid of spiders.
They creep me out the way they move.
They got hair and saliva. That's wrong.
A bug shouldn't have hair on it.

– Kevin Fitzgerald

CONTENTS

ACKNOWLEDGMENTS

I'm immensely grateful to my human clients, who asked questions and made comments that still make me laugh out loud years later. No, I will not name names to protect the innocently clueless. But you know who you are and how much I owe you, not just for these stories but also for my personal and professional growth.

I'd also like to thank all the furry and feathery patients who provided me with a lifetime of hilarious material for this and my future books. Without you constantly doing bizarre and inexplicable things, I would have had a much more boring career.

My deepest thanks go to my infinitely patient veterinary family who managed to keep straight faces during even the most ludicrous situations. From juggling scratching cats to dodging airborne bodily fluids, you rose to every challenge.

Finally, infinite gratitude to my amazingly understanding family for supporting my... calling, shall we say to veterinary comedy writing. Thank you for not disowning me when I spent our dinners comparing food to icky gooey bodily fluids or filled our shared Google drive with pictures of dog poop and puke.

While this book pokes fun at the humorous situations and comments from pet owners, rest assured that veterinarians themselves are not exempt from the jokes and amusing anecdotes. As the title suggests, I've experienced and told every conceivable joke about the ~~wet~~ vet life.

However, it's important to note that behind the laughter, veterinarians face significant emotional and mental challenges on a daily basis, leading to alarmingly high rates of depression and suicide in the profession. These funny stories are in no way intended to diminish or make light of the very real struggles that vets endure, including regular disrespect, difficult situations, burn-outs, imposter syndrome and mental breakdowns.

In fact, my goal with this humorous book is to shed more light on the realities of being a veterinarian. I hope to further explore the serious side of the profession, including the emotional toll it can take, in a future book that delves deeper into the harsh truths veterinarians often face behind the scenes.

Now let's dive into the hilarious and delightfully naive world of pet parents and their endearingly clueless enquiries about their furry and feathered companions.

PS- Reader's discretion advised. This book may be PG-13. Some words used in this book might be considered explicit even though they are a part of our daily lives, and these are genuine conversations that happened in the clinic.

Happy reading!

1

KIBBLES AND CRINGES: A CULINARY CONFUSION

KIBBLES

As a seasoned veterinarian, I've endured my fair share of peculiar client interactions. But every once in a while, a real doozy comes along that leaves you questioning the sanity of your chosen profession.

It began as a routine consultation about dog food options with a new pet parent. As I rattled off the pros and cons of various kibble brands, another client waiting nearby couldn't resist chiming in with their two cents.

"Oh no, don't go for Brand A," they interjected with unsolicited authority. "Brand B is much better. And Brand C tastes the best."

The pet parent's eyes widened, seemingly appreciative of the insider knowledge. "Oh, your pet finds this one tastier?" they asked innocently.

It was at this point that I began mentally drafting my letter of resignation from the veterinary field. For the intruding client responded without an iota of shame or self-awareness:

"No, I did. I try every food brand myself before giving it to my pet, and I found Brand C the tastiest."

All my surgical instruments could come together to cut through the awkwardness in that room at this revelation.

2

THE
CURIOUS CASE
OF THE
GENDER-CONFUSED
CANINE

It was a crisp summer morning when I found myself preparing for one of the most common operations in the veterinary field – rendering a ballsy dog, well, somewhat… less ballsy. As I prepared the operation theatre for the surgery, my client arrived with their beloved fur missile.

"So, doc," the well-meaning owner began, "I've got a question for you." I braced myself, having weathered many an odd inquiry over the years. But nothing could have prepared me for what came next.

"Will my dog become a female after this? When will he start having periods?" they asked with utterly sincere befuddlement.

I paused, pondering if I had heard correctly. Surely this was a joke. But the client's unwavering gaze confirmed a complete lack of guile behind the baffling question.

"He's male," I gently explained. "He won't have periods." A perfectly reasonable response, I thought. But I had sorely underestimated the creative mind before me.

"Yeah, but you're like taking away his balls, right? So won't that make him a female?" they doubled down, a hint of suspicion creeping into their voice.

At this point, I could hardly stifle my amusement. Peering down at the pup, I imagined him dolled up with a frilly pink collar, daintily crossing his legs while pensively awaiting his first moon cycle. The mere thought threatened to crumple my composure.

"Fear not," I managed after reining in my laughter. "Though we'll be... reshaping his manly physique today, Fido's core identity shall remain gloriously, undeniably male."

The client seemed semi-satisfied, though a glimmer of doubt still lurked behind their eyes. Nevertheless, we proceeded with the procedure, and in a few short hours, Fido emerged from my office – doggy dignity gloriously intact, yet infinitely more...relaxed in demeanour.

To this day, I can't resist a chuckle whenever I spot the beloved pup, miraculously un-ladylike, trotting along without a feminine care in the world. The mysteries of biology may forever elude some, but at least we can all revel in the delightfully awkward comedy of misconceptions.

3

THE CRIMSON CANINE CRISIS

whisper
100% STAIN PROTECTION
NOW FOR DOGS!

As a vet, you live for those priceless moments when a "pet emergency" devolves into an hilarious overreaction. Like the time the Oblivious clan called me at 8am, frantic.

"Doctor, you have to help! Coco is bleeding out!" Mrs. Oblivious wailed, her dramatics putting K Jo to shame. "She's dying!!"

I attempted to triage as Mr. O wrestled the phone away, pleading for an urgent visit. Visions of performing intense surgery danced in my head.

Moments later, they burst through the doors - Mr. O cradling their pet. It took thirty seconds to diagnose

Sadie's "horror" - a perfectly normal heat cycle.

You could literally hear the realization dawn on the Oblivious clan with an audible pop. As their faces cycled through the stages of grief, I stifled laughter.

They slunk away, vowing to better study pet womanhood.

Is there any greater honour than calming a code crimson period panic?

4

NEUTERING WOES AND MASCULINE AWOOS

Another day of reckoning for one bright-eyed pup whose unrestrained romancing had become a bit too...vigorous for the neighbourhood. As I prepared my tools and the anaesthetic, the dog's owner walked in, blissfully unaware of the impending brutality to come.

"So, doc, what exactly does 'neuter' mean?" they inquired with an air of nonchalance.

I cleared my throat, debating how delicately to phrase the upcoming procedure. "We'll be...castrating him."

The owner's brow furrowed in confusion. "What does that mean?"

So much for delicacy. "Uhm, we'll

be cutting off his testicles," I stated, embracing the blunt truth.

There was a prolonged silence as the words sank in. Then, as understanding dawned, the owner's face contorted into an expression of abject horror. Reflexively, their hands flew downward, cupping their own vulnerable manhood as if to protect it from my apparently savage practices.

"You're going to cut off his balls???" they yelped, voice escalating into a squeaky tone.

I sighed, wondering how this seemingly basic concept had evaded them for so long. "Well...yes, that's rather the essence of neutering. Like, what did you think was going to happen when you booked this appointment weeks ago?"

The owner's mouth opened and closed. At last, they managed a pitiful croak: "I...I thought you were just going to, you know...give him a shot or something!"

My shoulders sagged as I shook my head slowly. Clearly, the agonizing realities of pet population control had been utterly lost on this poor soul. Nevertheless, I pressed on - for the sake of preventing rampant puppy promiscuity.

When at last the valiant young lad roused from his slumber, still blissfully ignorant of his newly-absent appendages, the owner's traumatized expression said it all.

Neutering: somehow, it will never not be awkwardly emasculating for all involved.

5

THE FUR-LATHERING FIASCO

ORAL
USE
ONLY

As professionals in the pet care field, we've all endured our fair share of client misconceptions. But every once in a while, a real doozy comes along that leaves you questioning how the human race has sustained itself this long.

Enter Mr. Feisty-Fur, a particularly irate client who stormed into my clinic one afternoon, furry patient in tow. Barely suppressing his rage, he thrust the poor pup toward me.

"This medication you gave us isn't working!" he fumed, gesturing at the grease-matted disaster before us. "I've bathed her every day and it's done nothing!"

I examined the pup's stuck-together pelt and immediately suspected a grave mistake had been made. Treading lightly, I inquired, "How often are you administering the medication?"

Mr. F.F.'s face contorted like he'd bitten into a lemon. "I'm applying it all over him twice a day, just like you said!" he spat. "Do you know how many bottles I've gone through? How much money I've wasted on this junk?"

At that point, I had to stifle an unprofessional snort, lest I endure the wrath of a wronged pet owner. With exceeding care, I posed a clarifying question: "I'm so sorry, but...did you not read the dosage instructions?

The prescription states to give her 5ml of the syrup...orally?"

You could hear the veil lift from Mr. F.F.'s eyes as the horrible realization dawned. Like a kid caught varnishing the dog, he shrank back, cheeks flushing crimson. But of course, he couldn't admit fault so easily.

"Well maybe next time you should write that in bold!" he barked, refusing to go drown quietly.

I simply stood there, mouth agape as visions of a grown man squirting canine potions into his pup's topcoat replayed in my mind. How...how had we reached that point where spelling things out was necessary?

From then on, whenever I noticed an owner glazing over during dosage instructions, I made sure to reiterate in crisp, polished strokes:

"THE SYRUP IS TO BE INGESTED ORALLY, AS IN SWALLOWED WITH THE MOUTH, NOT APPLIED TOPICALLY." Because who knows how far a simple syrup misunderstanding could affect furred shoulders.

6

THE DELICATE DILEMMA OF THE DOGGY LIPSTICK

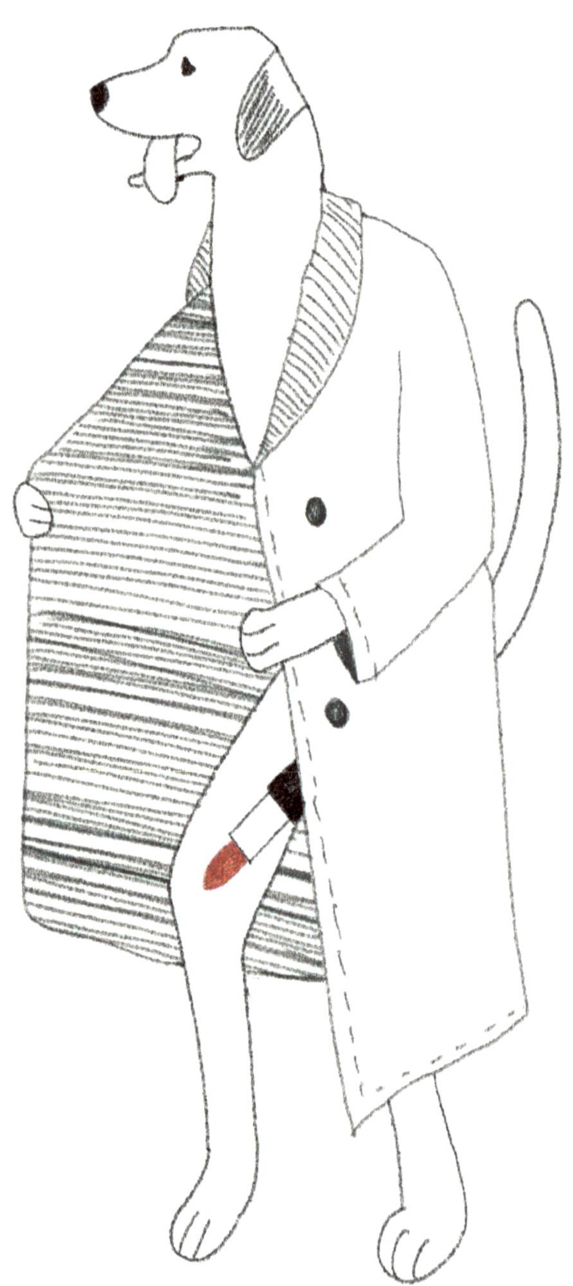

It began as any other routine visit to the veterinary clinic. I was preparing to examine the next patient when the owner strutted in, brow furrowed with apparent concern.

"Doc, I think my dog has a problem with his...red lipstick," they announced, voice lowered to an awkward half-whisper.

I paused, quirking one eyebrow quizzically. "I'm sorry, his what now?"

The owner seemed to shrink slightly, as if suddenly regretting their peculiar phrasing. "You know..." they pressed on, "His red lipstick...down there? The thing that peeps out of its cover?"

It took an excruciatingly elongated moment, but finally the punchline dawned on me. Struggling to stifle my amusement, I responded, "Ah, I think you mean his penis."

The words had barely left my mouth when the owner's face contorted into a horrified gasp. They recoiled, hands shooting up to dramatically cover my mouth. "Can you please not use such words out loud!" they hissed through gritted teeth, eyes frantically darting about to make sure no one else had heard me.

I gently removed their hands, struggling not to laugh at their thinly-veiled embarrassment.

Ah! The fun bits of being a vet.

7

ROOFIED RUFUS

BRUNO

It began with a frantic phone summons - a canine parent wailing that their pup, Rufus, was "acting super weird."

Finally, they burst in, Rufus lolling his tongue in blissful oblivion as his parents insisted on every test being conducted for the diagnosis of their precious baby at once.

With everything coming back normal, we tried to get a more detailed history as accusations of incompetence rained down upon us. That's when one whiff of the pup's dank aroma cleared the air - young Rufus's "erratic" behaviour stemmed from a certain herbal substance sampling.

Asrealizationdawnedonmycolleagues, I struggled not to snort-laugh at the entertainment that followed - the whiplash transformation from enraged customer to stammering adolescent as Rufus's human attempted to navigate this undeniable pickle in front of his mortified mother.

Somewhere between impassioned denials and desperate pleas of ignorance, all swagger drained from his demeanour.

In the end, we remedied Rufus while gently advising more discerning snacking habits for all involved.

From then on, any "weird" behaviour claim sparked a subtle nose-twitch from me, putting the team on high alert for any herbal high jinks afoot. You've got to hand it to dedicated pet parents - they really will go to crazy lengths to include their fur babies in every family pastime.

8

NIPPLE KNOWLEDGES

As a seasoned veterinarian, I've grown accustomed to clients' endearing ignorance about their pets' anatomy. So when an elderly gentleman requested I examine some "bumps" on his cat's lower body, I braced myself for another educational moment.

Upon inspection, the mysterious bumps revealed themselves to be nothing more than the feline's nipples. "Those are just his nipples," I explained matter-of-factly.

The client's eyes went wide with a mixture of confusion and doubt. "No, but he's a male," he protested firmly.

I couldn't help but chuckle at the fairytale notion that maleness and nipples were mutually exclusive traits. "Yes, males have nipples too," I gently clarified.

When the stubborn client refused to relent - "No, he's a male cat" - an unexpected voice pipes up from across the room.

"You're a male, but you have nipples too, right?" his wife chimed in with an impish grin. "The ones you like me to play with."

I very nearly swallowed my tongue. The ensuing silence hanged heavier than a herd of constipated elephants, broken only by my desperate wheezing as I frantically gasped for professionalism.

From then on, whenever I've spied a client's nipular areas, I've been unable to bypass the previous incident's cursed visuals. Who knew the human body contained such horrors?

9

THE PERILS OF PAWS AND CLAWS

O₂ - 9

In our bustling clinic, emergencies were a daily affair. One such night, a frantic couple burst through the doors, clutching their beloved pooch, Rover, who was bleeding profusely from his mouth.

"Save him, Doctor! He's our everything!" they cried, tears streaming down their faces.

I nodded solemnly, ushering them to the treatment room. But as I prepared for the treatment, the couple made an unexpected request.

"Doc, while you're at it, could you trim his nails and give him a little haircut? He's a bit of a diva, you see. Won't let us near him with clippers!"

I blinked, incredulous. "Of course, because nothing says 'emergency' like a fresh new do!"

And thus, amidst the chaos of saving Rover's life, we found ourselves juggling scalpels and scissors, muttering sarcastic remarks under our breath. For in the world of veterinary medicine, even in the face of peril, there's always room for a little comedy – and a lot of love for our furry friends.

10

PUPPY PLAYTHINGS

100%
Durable
Rope

As a veterinary professional, I've learned to expect the occasional off-the-wall client request. But one incident left me wishing I'd chosen a different career path entirely.

It started innocently enough when a client asked about toys for her male dog. "We have plenty of options in our pet store," I offered helpfully.

The woman frowned. "No, there are no toys for male dogs."

Red flag number one. I treaded cautiously. "Did you have something specific in mind?"

And that's when she dropped the bombshell: "Yes, the ones he can hump and masturbate with."

"We...don't carry those..." I choked out, clinging to my last shreds of professionalism.

But she was relentless. "Why not? Dogs need sex toys too! Don't we girls know the importance of a good toy!!"

I stood there, mouth agape.

From then on, I couldn't so much as glance at our toy aisle without rehashing that traumatic conversation - the notion of canines and... recreation devices dancing in my mind's eye.

11

A HARD PILL TO FIND

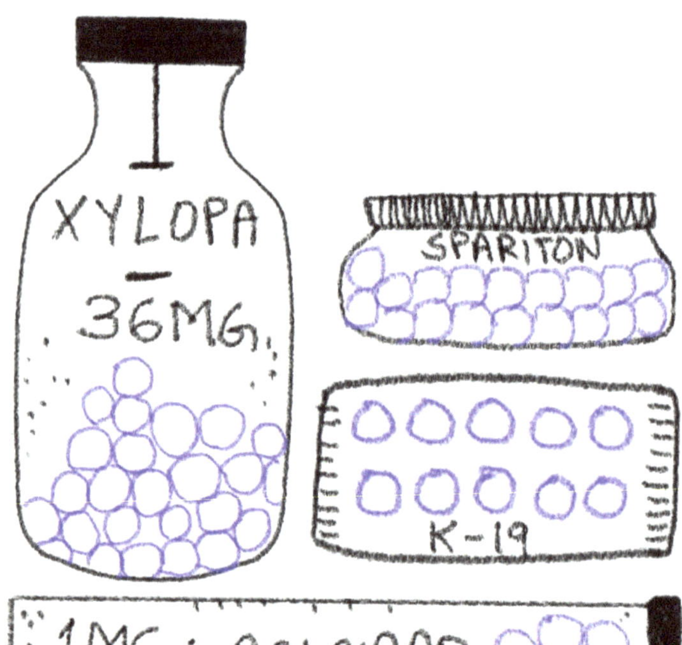

XYLOPA
36MG.
SPARITON
K-19
1MG: CALCIPAR

In the bustling corridors of our vet clinic, every request brought its own flavour of absurdity. One day, a client strolled in with a perplexing dilemma.

"I need a refill for my pet's meds," they declared, a hint of urgency in their voice.

Our receptionist nodded, ever the picture of professionalism. "Of course. What's the name of the medication?"

The client paused, scratching their head. "Ah, you see, I seem to have misplaced the prescription. But I do remember it was a small, white, round pill."

Our receptionist's eyebrow arched in disbelief. "Oh, well, that narrows it down a lot," she deadpanned, unable to resist a touch of sarcasm.

And so, amidst the sea of vague descriptions and misplaced documents, the hunt for the elusive medication began. For in the world of pet care, even the simplest tasks can turn into a wild goose chase – with a healthy dose of humour along the way.

12

THE DREADED "ASKING FOR A FRIEND" FAUX PAS

We've all had one of those calls - the ones that make you question why you pursued this career path to begin with. For me, it went a little something like this:

"Sorry if this sounds weird, but I have to ask you something," the caller prefaced ominously. "It's for a friend."

I steeled myself, figuring it was another case of feigning plausible deniability. "Sure, go ahead."

"It's for a friend," they reiterated slowly, as if afraid I'd missed that crucial detail. "Just so you know."

Fighting a smirk, I assured them, "Okay, I get it. What's the question?"

There was a pause, presumably as they psyched themselves up for the impending words.

"Can a human get pregnant if they have sex with a dog? Asking for a friend."

You could've heard my soul exit my body.

From then on, whenever someone utters that ominous friend-related disclaimer, I can't help but brace for the unholiest of anatomical inquiries. Humans, am I right? We really are the most eccentric species on this planet.

13

A DOG'S EXPENSIVE TASTE

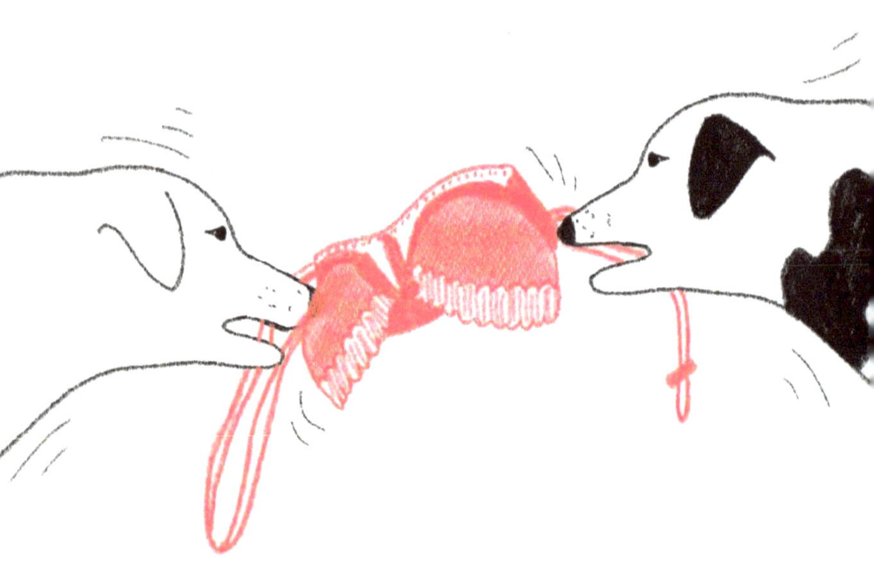

Mrs. S rushed her beloved pooch, Buddy, to the vet after he had been vomiting for days. The diagnosis? Buddy had swallowed a "foreign object" that needed surgical removal from his stomach.

During the operation, the vet chuckled as he pulled out the culprit – a lacy, expensive bra belonging to Mrs. S herself. Apparently, Buddy had developed a taste for high-end lingerie.

When Mrs. S received the vet bill, she insisted on a discount, claiming, "That was a brand-new bra, and since you found and kept it, I should at least get the cost deducted from the surgery!"

The vet, amused by her audacity, could only shake his head and remind her that a dog's idea of a delicacy often differs from our own.

14

FROM
PAW TO
PAW-RENTHOOD

Sperm

There were rumours flying around about certain breeds being banned, with the news popping up regular articles on these breeds and their violent behaviour.

Amidst these rumours, we get a call from a client who had quite the demand for us.

"Hey, do you guys help in extracting sperm?" he enquired.

I stood there bamboozled, wondering how to respond to that particular query, finally compromising by asking him to repeat himself, hoping he would realise he has called a Vet clinic and not a "sample donation" place.

"You know, helping my dog masturbate and then collecting his sperm?" the unfazed client replied.

It took me all my will power to keep s straight face as I informed him, we did not provide those "services" here.

Out of curiosity, I decided to further enquire about the reason behind such needs arising.

"Oh, if they ban his breed, I want to make sure I have some of his sperm frozen to continue his lineage."

It took me quite some time to explain the true meaning of a breed ban to him.

15

THE MYSTERIOUS COCO

COCO
COCO
COCO

In veterinary clinics, every pet has a story – and sometimes, a touch of mystery. One sunny afternoon, a frazzled client dialled the clinic's number, seeking crucial information about their beloved Coco.

"Hello," they began, their tone brimming with urgency. "I need to know when Coco's vaccines are due."

I, ever the picture of patience, dove into the conversation with enthusiasm. "Absolutely, we're happy to help. Can we have some more details about Coco?"

The client hesitated, as if caught off guard by the request. "Well, she's

Coco," they insisted, as if that were all the information needed in the world.

But I knew better. "We have around 200 Cocos in our records," I explained gently. "Could you provide a bit more detail?"

Suddenly, the conversation took an unexpected turn. The client's patience wore thin, and accusations flew like catnip at a feline fiesta.

"I don't like your tone," they declared, their voice tinged with indignation. "You're being unhelpful on purpose!"

With that, they threatened to unleash the wrath of the internet, vowing to leave a scathing Google review that would echo through the annals of cyberspace.

And just like that, the line went dead, leaving me to ponder the enigma of Coco – and the curious case of a client with a penchant for drama.

For in the world of pet care, even the simplest requests can spiral into the threat of an online review.

ABOUT THE AUTHOR

Dr. Jasleen Kaur is a practicing Veterinary Surgeon and Radiologist, who along with being a Vet, holds a Diploma in Animal Protection Laws from NALSAR University and has also done her Post Graduate Programme in Management for Working Professionals from Indian School of Business, majoring in Marketing.

Dr. Jasleen has grown up around dogs, and vowed to become a Vet when she lost her first pet at the age of 13. After working in different practices and moving on further studies post her graduation in 2013, she started her own practice in 2017.

Following her personal beliefs that pet care starts at home, her practice focuses primarily on compassionate and ethical treatment of pets, along with client education.

Dr. Jasleen also manages her Instagram page **jasleenspetcare** where she talks about pet care and mental health in the Veterinary field.

www.ingramcontent.com/pod-product-compliance
Lightning Source LLC
Chambersburg PA
CBHW040954110726

48007CB00004B/30